Living Habitats

Living in the

Heinemann Library
Chicago, Illinois

Carol Baldwin

Customer Service 888-454-2279

Visit our website at www.heinemannlibrary.com

Designed by Kimberly Saar, Heinemann Library
Illustrations and maps by John Fleck
Photo research by Alan Gottlieb
Printed and bound in the United States by Lake Book Manufacturing, Inc.

08 07 06 05 04
10 9 8 7 6 5 4 3 2 1

Library of Congress Cataloging-in-Publication Data
Baldwin, Carol, 1943-
   Living in the taiga / Carol Baldwin.
      v. cm. -- (Living habitats)
Contents: What makes land taiga? -- Why is the taiga important? -- What's green and growing in the taiga? -- What animals live in the taiga? -- How do animals live in the taiga? -- What's for dinner in the taiga? -- How do taiga animals get food? -- How does the taiga affect people? -- How do the people affect the taiga?
   ISBN 1-4034-2994-4 (lib. bdg.) -- ISBN 1-4034-3236-8 (pbk.)
   1. Taigas--Juvenile literature. [1. Taiga ecology. 2. Taigas. 3. Ecology.] I. Title
   QH86.B365 2003
   577.3'7--dc21

                        2003001543

Acknowledgments
The author and publishers are grateful to the following for permission to reproduce copyright material:
pp. 4, 5, 8 Bryan & Cherry Alexander; p. 6 Courtesy Martin Guitar; p. 7 Kevin Schafer/Corbis; p. 9 Stephen J. Krasemann/Photo Researchers, Inc.; p. 10 Hal Horwitz/Corbis; p. 11a S. R. Maglione/Photo Researchers, Inc.; p. 12 Roger Wilmshurst/Photo Researchers, Inc.; p. 13 Maslowski/Photo Researchers, Inc.; p. 14 Art Wolfe/Photo Researchers, Inc.; p. 15 Robert J.Erwin/Photo Researchers, Inc.; p. 16 Joe McDonald/Corbis; p. 17 Jen & Des Bartlett/Bruce Coleman Inc.; p. 18 Stephen P. Parker/Photo Researchers, Inc.; p. 19 Phil Degginger/Bruce Coleman Inc.; p. 20 Alan Carey/Photo Researchers, Inc.; p. 21 Bill Banaszewski/Visuals Unlimited; p. 22 D. Robert & Lorri Franz/Corbis; p. 24 Bryan & Cherry Alexander/Photo Researchers, Inc.; p. 25 Gunter Marx Photography/Corbis; p. 26 Stuart Westmorland/Photo Researchers, Inc.; p. 27 Richard Price/Getty Images.

Cover photograph by Charles Mauzy/Corbis

About the cover: Taiga is also a type of biome. It is the largest terrestrial biome on Earth.

Every effort has been made to contact copyright holders of any material reproduced in this book. Any omissions will be rectified in subsequent printings if notice is given to the publisher.

Some words are shown in bold, **like this**. You can find out what they mean by looking in the glossary.

Contents

1 What Makes Land Taiga?

Tall spruce and fir trees tower around you. A layer of needlelike leaves cushions your feet as you walk. This **habitat** is the taiga.

The taiga is a northern forest

Most taiga is in Alaska, Canada, Scandinavia, and Siberia. It is also called boreal forest or northern coniferous forest. Most taiga trees are **conifers.**

By the end of November, most of the taiga is covered by more than a foot (0.3 meters) of snow.

Winters are long and cold

Winter temperatures often drop below −40 °F (−40 °C). The taiga gets 16 to 40 inches (40 to 100 centimeters) of **precipitation** each year. Most of this falls as snow. Snow covers the ground for four to six months of the year. Lakes are ice covered in winter. Summers are short and cool. Temperatures rarely get above 68 °F (20 °C).

? Did you know?

The word boreal comes from Boreas, the Greek god of the north wind. Taiga is a Russian word for marshy forest.

Soils are thin and poor

Thousands of years ago, **glaciers** covered parts of Earth. These huge ice sheets scraped away the taiga soil. When these glaciers melted, only bare rock was left. New soil forms slowly, and dead plants and animals decay slowly in cold weather. So the thin soil has few **nutrients.** Conifer leaves make the soil acidic. Many plants cannot grow in acid soil.

Much land is covered with lakes and bogs

Glaciers also scraped holes in the land as they moved. When the glaciers melted, the holes filled with water to become lakes and ponds.

In northern Russia, **conifers,** lakes, ponds, and bogs stretch for more than 9,000 miles.

Grasslike plants grew around the edges of the water. As the plants died, they fell into the cold water. They never decayed. Over time, they built up into deep layers of **peat.** Many ponds filled in completely to form soft, spongy ground called **bogs.**

2 Why Is the Taiga Important?

Although the taiga is a cold **habitat,** many plants and animals live there. Few people live there, but we all use its **resources.**

People use taiga trees

Some companies cut pine trees for lumber to make floors and furniture. Others cut spruces, firs, jack pines, and aspens for **pulpwood.** Logs are ground into pulp to make paper. Pines are used to make railroad ties and telephone poles. Spruce wood is also used to make stringed musical instruments, such as guitars, violins, and cellos. **Resin** from fir and larch trees is used to make turpentine. Resin from fir trees is also used to make a product that glues pieces of glass together to make lenses for glasses. The bark of hemlock trees is used for tanning leather.

Spruce wood is often used to make the sounding boards of musical instruments.

The taiga is home for living things

The taiga does not have as many kinds of plants as some other habitats. But many animals do live in this harsh land. Large animals that live in the taiga include bears, moose, and wolves. Small animals include birds, squirrels, chipmunks, and mice.

In addition to trees, mosses and **lichens** are **adapted** to the taiga. They grow thickly on the forest floor and on the branches and trunks of trees. Grasslike sedges grow around lakes, ponds, and **bogs.** Wildflowers and a few bushes grow in other areas.

A few people live in the taiga

Most people do not live in the taiga all year. They spend only summers there, hunting or herding reindeer. Then, they move north to the treeless **tundra** in summer.

The spruce grouse lives across Canada in spruce, larch, pine, and juniper forests. Most of the grouse's diet is made up of evergreen needles and buds.

3 What's Green and Growing in the Taiga

The taiga is a forest **habitat,** so most of the plants growing there are trees. However, other plants grow there too.

Conifers

Conifers are **adapted** to living in the taiga. Their trunks grow straight. Branches grow out from the trunks like spokes on a wheel. The branches can bend easily. Conifers' needlelike leaves have a waxy coating that keeps them from drying out in the cold wind. Trees also grow close together and protect one another from winter winds. Cones protect the trees' seeds.

Conifer root systems are shallow because the soil is thin. There are very few **nutrients** in the soil. But **fungi** growing around their roots can make nutrients for the trees. In return, the fungi get food made by the trees' leaves.

Because conifer branches bend easily, heavy snow can slide off without breaking them.

8

White spruce and black spruce are the two main trees found throughout the taiga. Other species of trees also grow in the taiga. Jack pines are common in western North America. Balsam firs are in eastern North America. Larches are the most common taiga conifers in eastern Asia. They are unusual because they shed their leaves in winter. The leaves turn yellow or red before they drop. In parts of the taiga, pines also mix with spruces.

Other trees

Aspen, birch, and alder are taiga trees that produce seeds in fruits. They grow in areas that have been cleared by forest fires and fallen or logged trees. Birches also grow on the northern edges of the taiga. Aspens grow throughout this habitat. Alders grow in wetter areas. They're often found near ponds, **bogs,** and on riverbanks.

Many animals eat the seeds, leaves, buds, and twigs of birch and aspen trees.

9

Nodding trilliums grow well in the damp, acidic soils of the coniferous forest.

Plants of the forest floor

The forest floor below the spruces and firs is dark. Not much light can reach through the thick tree branches. More sunlight reaches the floor below pines and larches. Their branches do not block as much light. The floor is also littered with needlelike leaves. Ferns and mosses grow well in dim, damp areas. Where the ground is drier and gets more sunlight, grasses grow.

Wildflowers such as mayflowers, white violets, and trilliums also grow in sunny areas. And bushes like highbush cranberry, elderberry, and blueberry grow there, too. **Lichens** also grow on rocks and trees in the forest.

Lichens

A lichen isn't a plant. It's a **fungus** and an **alga** that live together. The fungus clings to rocks or trees. The alga makes food for them both. Alone, the fungus would starve and the alga would be blown away by strong wind.

Bog and muskeg plants

Muskegs are areas of wet **peat** with trees and shrubs growing on them. In these areas, trees such as tamarack, black spruce, and cedar are found. But they don't grow very tall. Many are no more than about 15 feet (4.6 meters) tall.

Pitcher plants capture and digest insects because they cannot get enough **nutrients** from the soil.

Many plants cannot grow in **bogs** because they are too wet. But sphagnum mosses thrive in wet, acidic water. Grasslike sedges and pitcher plants also grow well in taiga bogs and peatlands. Pitcher plants are **carnivorous** bog plants. Their long, trumpet-shaped leaves collect rainwater and other liquids. Insects crawl into the "pitchers." But downward-pointing hairs keep them from crawling back out. The insects are trapped in the pool of water and drown. The plant then takes in nutrients from the insects' bodies.

4 What Animals Live in the Taiga?

The taiga is home to a variety of large animals. But they are spread out over wide areas, so you might have a hard time finding them. You would be more likely to see small animals, birds, and insects.

Mammals

Red foxes are mammals that are most active at dawn and dusk. But sometimes you might spot one during the day. You would notice its reddish coat and long, bushy, white-tipped tail. If you saw a brown animal about the size of a horse, it could be a moose. Male moose have large, flat antlers that drop off in winter. Moose are strong, fast swimmers.

Other large mammals include grizzly bears, wolves, lynxes, woodland caribou, and wolverines. Small taiga mammals include snowshoe hares, red squirrels, Siberian chipmunks, voles, and deer mice.

Red squirrels live in the coniferous forests of Europe and Asia. Sharp, hooklike claws help them cling to tree trunks.

Birds

Some taiga birds, such as crossbills, boreal chickadees, and woodpeckers live in trees. Crossbills feed on **conifer** seeds. Chickadees feed on seeds, berries, and insects. Three-toed and great spotted woodpeckers use their strong bills to chip open tree bark. Then they use their long tongues to gather insect **larvae** from just under the bark.

This red crossbill uses its beak to pry open the scales of a cone and pull out the seeds.

Other taiga birds live on the forest floor. Spruce grouse, turkeys, and hazel grouse feed on berries, buds, seeds, and insects. Capercailles are turkeylike birds that live in the taiga of Europe and Asia. They feed on berries, grass, and the buds and young shoots of conifers.

Other taiga birds, such as great gray owls, eagle owls, gyrfalcons, and goshawks, are fierce hunters. They fly through the air or perch in trees watching for food.

13

The luna moth has wings that can measure up to 4 inches (11 centimeters) across. They live only about two weeks because they have no mouth parts and can't eat. However, their caterpillars munch the leaves of birches and other trees.

Reptiles and Amphibians

Most reptiles and amphibians are not able to live in cold **habitats** like the taiga. However, a few can. During summer you might see reptiles such as garter snakes and snapping turtles. You might also see such amphibians as boreal chorus frogs and wood frogs. The frogs stay close to ponds, **bogs,** and lakes.

Insects

Many insects live in the taiga. Mosquitoes, deerflies, wasps, and bees buzz through the forest. Colorful dragonflies, butterflies, and moths fly about through the trees. Caterpillars of monarch and mourning cloak butterflies crawl on plants. And insect pests, such as spruce budworms, dig holes deep into trees, harming them.

How Do Animals Live in the Taiga?

Some animals are **adapted** to live in the taiga all year long. Others live there only in summer or winter.

Some animals migrate

Some animals spend only summers in the taiga. They **migrate** from farther south. Ducks, geese, juncos, and yellow-bellied sapsuckers are birds that breed and nest in the taiga. In fall, they go back south.

Western tanagers breed in the Canadian taiga, but migrate to Mexico in winter.

Other animals, such as barren-ground caribou, spend only winters in the taiga. In summer, they migrate farther north to the treeless **tundra.** As winter approaches, they move south to the taiga. Some wolf packs also migrate to follow the caribou. A few birds, such as redpolls, also migrate north from the taiga in summer.

> **? Did you know?**
> Woodland caribou are smaller than barren-ground caribou found in the tundra. They are an **endangered** species that lives year round only in the taiga.

A chipmunk makes a bed of shredded grass and leaves in its burrow. It also stores food there because it wakes up from time to time during its winter hibernation.

Some animals hibernate

Some taiga animals **hibernate** through cold winters. A hibernating animal goes into a deep sleep. To get ready for winter, it eats a lot of food. It will use stored body fat as food. A **burrow** protects it from the cold. Chipmunks, ground squirrels, and woodchucks are taiga mammals that hibernate. Some reptiles also hibernate in the taiga. Snapping turtles hibernate by burrowing in mud at the bottom of ponds and lakes. Hundreds of garter snakes hibernate together in underground dens.

Do bears hibernate?

Bears, along with skunks, raccoons, and opossums, do not really hibernate. Their body temperatures drop a few degrees and their heart rates slow down. But they wake up easily if they are disturbed.

Some animals store food

Some birds that are in the taiga all winter store food. In fall, white-breasted nuthatches store seeds in cracks in tree bark. During summer, blue jays and Steller's jays bury extra seeds and nuts in the ground to save for winter.

A beaver's thick, waterproof fur keeps it dry in the water.

Some mammals also store food for winter. Beavers build lodges, or houses, of sticks and mud in the middle of ponds or streams. Underwater tunnels lead to the living area. During winter, beavers feed on bark, twigs, and leaves inside their lodges.

Some animals live under the winter snow

Some mice and their relatives, voles, dig tunnels under the winter snow. They travel through them to search for seeds and stems on the forest floor.

❓ Did you know?

Many insects spend the winter as **pupae,** either buried deep in the ground or inside tree trunks.

6 What's for Dinner in the Taiga?

All living things need food. Some living things, like plants, can make their own food. But animals need to find and eat food to live.

Plants

Plants make, or produce, their own food. So they are called **producers.** Plants like trees, bushes, ferns, mosses, wildflowers, and sedges are producers that grow in the taiga. They make food from carbon dioxide gas in the air and water from their roots. Plants need energy to change the carbon dioxide and water into sugars. The energy comes from sunlight. This process of making food is called **photosynthesis.**

Highbush blueberries and other bushes are taiga producers. Blueberries are eaten by many birds, small mammals, and bears.

Did you know?

Not all producers are plants. **Algae** that are part of **lichens** are producers. But they belong to a group of living things called **protists.**

Animals

Animals are called **consumers** because they eat, or consume, food. Some taiga animals eat only plants. These animals are called **herbivores.** Moose, porcupines, caterpillars, and capercaillies are some taiga herbivores. Other animals eat both plants and animals. They are called **omnivores.** Wolverines, voles, and red foxes are omnivores. Still others, such as lynxes, great gray owls, and goshawks, eat only animals. These animals are **carnivores.**

In summer, moose often wade into lakes to feed on water plants.

The clean-up crew

Decomposers feed on dead plants and animals and their wastes. **Bacteria, molds,** and some beetles are decomposers. Decomposers break down **nutrients** stored in dead plants and animals. They put them back into the soil, air, and water. Plants use the nutrients to help them grow. The needlelike leaves of **conifers** take a long time to break down. That's why the forest floor is covered with them.

7 How Do Taiga Animals Get Food?

Some taiga animals hunt for food. Others **forage** or **scavenge** for food.

Hunting

Animals that hunt and kill other animals for food are **predators.** Lynxes are predators. They catch and eat hares, mice, small deer, and grouse. Red-backed voles eat fruits, berries, and grasses. But they also hunt and eat insects. So both lynxes and voles are predators. Animals that predators eat are **prey.** Mice and deer are prey of lynxes.

The taiga **bogs** and ponds are great breeding grounds for insects during the summer. Many birds, such as spruce grouse, boreal chickadees, blue jays, gray jays, and pine grosbeaks feed on these insects. Woodpeckers hunt and eat insects and their **larvae** that live in trees. So, insect-eating birds are also predators.

> Sounds in the dense forest do not travel well. The tufts on a lynx's ears help it hear better. This helps it find prey.

Some taiga animals are both predators and prey. Voles eat insects. So sometimes they are predators. However, voles are also eaten by great gray owls and red foxes. So, they are also prey. Spruce grouse sometimes eat insects. So, sometimes they are predators. However, goshawks hunt and eat the grouse. So, grouse are also prey.

Foraging

Animals such as moose, caribou, elk, hares, and capercaillies are **foragers.** They move about, sometimes in groups, to search for food. Capercaillies forage on flowers and berries in summer. But in winter they move through the trees and forage on pine needles and cones.

Elk, called red deer in Europe, live in more open parts of the forest. Their favorite foods are found around bogs.

Elk forage on sedges and other bog plants. They also forage on grasses and the shoots of bushes and trees.

Scavenging

Sometimes animals die of old age or illness. **Scavengers** are animals that eat the bodies of animals that are already dead. Food is harder to find in winter. Prey animals may be **hibernating** or may have **migrated.** So, some **predators** will become scavengers. Wolves, wolverines, and grizzly bears will **scavenge.**

A wolverine is a strong hunter. But in winter, it mainly scavenges animals, such as elk, caribou, and deer. Its keen sense of smell lets it find animals even buried under heavy snow.

Grizzly bears sometimes bury the leftovers of a large animal that they have killed. They return later to feed on the remains. However, wolverines or eagles may scavenge the body before the grizzly returns.

A wolverine's strong jaws allow it to eat even the frozen body of a dead animal.

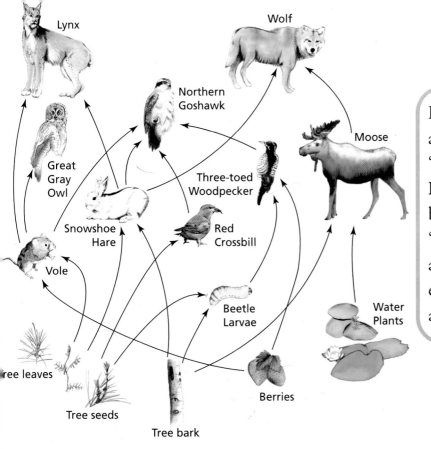

Lynx

Wolf

Northern Goshawk

Great Gray Owl

Moose

Three-toed Woodpecker

Snowshoe Hare

Red Crossbill

Vole

Beetle Larvae

Water Plants

Tree leaves

Tree seeds

Berries

Tree bark

In a food web, an arrow is drawn from "dinner" to the "diner." **Producers** are on the bottom of the web. "Top" predators, animals that no one else hunts and eats, are at the top.

Planning the menu

The path that shows who eats what in a **habitat** is a **food chain.** All living things are parts of food chains. In the taiga, red-backed voles feed on leaves of fir and spruce trees. Great gray owls eat the voles.

Another taiga food chain includes snowshoe hares that feed on berries and grasses. Snowshoe hares are eaten by lynxes. A third taiga food chain includes water plants, moose, and wolves. All the food chains that are connected in a habitat make up a **food web.** Many living things in a food web are part of more than one food chain.

8 How Does the Taiga Affect People?

Groups of **native peoples** live in the taiga. However, most do not live there all year. But the taiga even affects people who don't live there at all.

Many native people move around

In Canada, native people such as the Cree and the Innu live in the taiga. They depend on the forests, the waters, and other natural **resources.** In Scandinavia and Russia, many native people spend only winters in the taiga. The Sami people of Scandinavia and the Nenets of Siberia are nomads. They spend winters in the taiga with their reindeer herds. They also hunt and fish in the forests. In summer they move north to the treeless **tundra.** There, the reindeer graze on **lichens.** The people also hunt and fish there.

The culture of the Nenets stresses respect for the land and its resources. They use only what they need from the taiga.

The forest provides jobs

Jobs provided by logging, papermaking, home building, and furniture making depend on the taiga trees. Other jobs depend on recreation in the forests. Fishing guides help people find the best places to fish in the taiga's lakes. Game wardens make sure that people follow the hunting and fishing laws.

The thick bark of many trees can protect them from small fires. When trees are killed, other trees grow to replace them.

Forest fires destroy buildings

Many forest fires are started by lightning, but some are started by people. Dry needles and branches on the ground burn easily when there is no snow cover. But fires can actually help the forest. Fires get rid of ground litter in the forest. And the cones of some trees need fire to make them open and release their seeds. However, when people build homes and other buildings in the forest, fires can destroy them.

9 How Do People Affect the Taiga?

Not many people live in the taiga. But people still have an effect on the **habitat.**

People cut many trees

Many **conifer** trees are cut for use in making paper. Lumber and paper companies have logged large areas of taiga. Cutting all the trees in part of a forest is called clear-cutting. When trees are cut, plants, animals, and **native peoples** lose their homes. Scientists worry that in the harsh climate, trees in clear-cut areas may never grow back. Without trees, rain washes away soil.

As people use more and more paper, more areas of the taiga may disappear.

People mine

Much of the taiga contains large deposits of **minerals,** such as gold and iron. Mines dug to reach the minerals are big, open pits. Roads and railroads are built to carry the minerals out. Large areas of habitat are lost. **Pollution** from mining harms water and land.

People cause acid rain

Pollution from power plants and other industries can travel hundreds of miles. It mixes with water vapor in clouds. Rain or snow that falls from these clouds is acidic. When it falls on taiga trees, it damages their leaves. It also harms their roots when it soaks into the soil. In some parts of Scandinavia and Russia, large parts of the taiga have died from acid rain.

People protect the taiga

Some parts of the taiga are now protected as parks. Large areas in Canada and Russia are protected. Sir Winston Churchill Provincial Park in Alberta, Canada, and Russia's Kostomukshshkiy Nature Reserve are two such protected areas. However, more taiga needs to be protected. Many parts are still threatened by logging, mining, and road building.

National parks in the Canadian taiga protect the habitat for the future.

Fact File

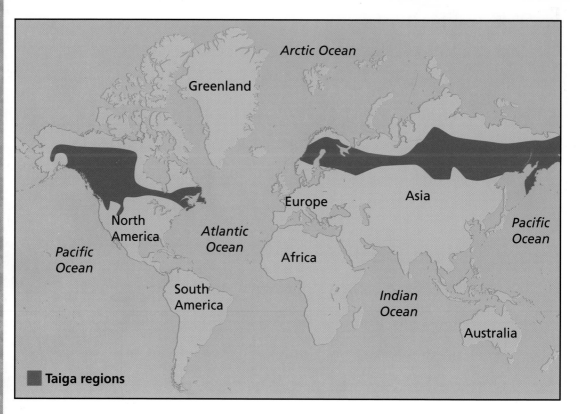

Taiga regions

Taiga Rescue Network

In 1992, the Taiga Rescue Network (TRN) was established. More than 150 organizations belong to the group. North America is represented by the Boreal Forest Network. TRN works to make sure that development does not harm the native people who live in the taiga. Many of them continue to live in the traditional way. TRN is supporting the Sami in Sweden as they fight for the right to use traditional grazing areas for their reindeer. Private land owners are trying to use the land for themselves.

Taiga's trees

Name	Uses by people	Uses by wildlife
white spruce	pulp to make paper, shipping crates	Grouse and other birds eat the seeds; porcupines eat the bark.
black spruce	pulp, fuel	Squirrels eat the seeds; hares eat young trees.
balsam fir	pulp, crates, boxes	Moose and deer eat the needles and twigs; chickadees, nutcrackers, squirrels, and porcupines eat the seeds; spruce grouse eat the needles.
tamarack (larch)	poles, railroad ties	Deer browse young trees; porcupines eat the inner bark; squirrels, mice, chipmunks, and crossbills eat the seeds.
jack pine	pulp, poles	Hares and porcupines eat young trees; porcupines eat the bark; squirrels, mice, chipmunks, goldfinches, and other birds eat the seeds.
Norway spruce	pulp, furniture, musical instruments	Hares eat young trees; deer feed on the bark; grouse eat the needles; small mammals and birds eat the seeds.
white pine	house frames, cabinets	Crossbills, chickadees, and other birds eat the seeds; beavers, porcupines, and hares feed on the bark and twigs; squirrels, chipmunks, and mice eat the seeds.
quaking aspen	crates, boxes, fences	Beavers, bears, and moose, eat the twigs and leaves; many birds eat the buds, and seeds.
paper birch	pulp	Moose and deer browse on twigs; beavers feed on the inner bark; grouse eat the buds; small birds and mammals eat the tiny seeds.
speckled alder	none	Grouse eat the buds; rabbits, deer, and moose eat the twigs.
balsam poplar	pulp, crates, boxes	Grouse and other birds eat the buds and twigs; moose browse the twigs and leaves; beavers, hares, squirrels, and porcupines eat the buds, bark, and leaves.

Glossary

adapted changed to live under certain conditions

alga (plural: **algae**) producer that lives in damp places

bacteria living things too small to be seen except with a microscope.

bog patch of ground that is always wet and spongy

burrow hole dug in the ground by animals for shelter

carnivore animal that eats only other animals

carnivorous eating only other animals

conifer trees that make their seeds in cones

consumer living thing that needs plants for food

decomposer organism that breaks down and dead plants and animals puts nutrients from them back into the soil, air, and water

endangered animals or plants that might all die (become extinct)

food chain path that shows who eats what in a habitat

food web group of connected food chains in a habitat

forage wander about in search of food

forager animal or person that wanders about searching for food

fungus (plural: **fungi**) living thing that feeds on dead or living plant or animal matter. Mushrooms and molds are fungi.

glacier large, slow-moving sheet of ice

habitat place where a plant or animal lives

herbivore animals that eats only plants

hibernate spend the winter in a state in which an animal's body greatly slows down

larvae young of insects

lichen living thing made of an alga and fungi that live together

migrate move from place to place with the seasons

mineral any material dug from the earth by mining. Gold, iron, and diamonds are minerals.

mold living thing that uses dead plants and animals for food. Molds are decomposers.

native people people who have lived in an area for a very long time and whose anscestors were born there

nomads people who move around from place to place

nutrient material that is needed for the growth of a plant or animal

omnivore animals that eats plants and animals

peat spongy mass made mostly of unrotted plant material

photosynthesis proces by which green plants trap the sun's energy and use it to change carbon dioxide and water into sugars

pollution harmful materials in the water, air, or land

precipitation rain, snow, sleet, or hail

predator animal that hunts and eats other animals

prey animal that is hunted and eaten by other animals

producer living thing that can use sunlight to make its own food

protist type of living thing that is neither a plant nor an animal. Algae are protists.

pulpwood any soft wood that can be used to make paper

pupae stage of insect life between larvae and adults. A pupa is sometimes called a chrysalis.

resin sticky, yellowish substance that flows from conifer trees

resource anything that meets a need that people, plants, or animals have

scavenge feed on the bodies of dead animals

scavenger animal that eats the bodies of animals that are already dead

tundra cold, treeless area

More Books to Read

Breining, Greg. *The Northern Forest*. New York: Benchmark Books, 2000.

Johnson, Rebecca L. *A Walk in the Boreal Forest*. Minneapolis, Minn.: Carolrhoda Books, 2001.

Pipes, Rose. *Forests and Woodlands*. Austin, Tex.: Raintree/Steck-Vaughn, 1999.

Index

THEY
ALSO
SERVED

THEY
ALSO
SERVED

Baseball and the Home Front,
1941–1945

BILL GILBERT

CROWN PUBLISHERS, INC.
NEW YORK

T O   L I L L I A N   A N D   D A V E
A N D   T O   S H I R L E Y   P O V I C H

Grateful acknowledgment is made to the following for permission to reprint previously published material: Warner/Chappell Music, Inc. and Polygram/ Island Music Publishing Group for an excerpt from "Johnny Zero" written by Mack David and Vee Lawnhurst. Copyright © 1943 by Chappell & Co. & Alta Music Corp. Copyright © 1943 Polygram International Publishing, Inc. All rights administered by Chappell & Co. and Polygram/Island Music Publishing Group. All rights reserved. CPP Belwin, Inc. for an excerpt from "Comin' In On A Wing And A Prayer" by Jimmy McHugh and Harold Adamson. Copyright © 1943 Robbins Music Corporation. Renewed 1971 Robbins Music Corporation and Jimmy McHugh Music Inc. Rights for Robbins Music Corporation assigned to EMI Catalog Partnership and controlled and administered by EMI Robbins Catalog Inc. International copyright secured. Made in USA. All rights reserved. Herman Helms and the Columbia, S.C. State for Roberto Ortiz story and "Yellow Dog." Richard Goldstein for excerpts from SPARTAN SEASONS: HOW BASEBALL SURVIVED THE SECOND WORLD WAR. Copyright © 1980 by Richard Goldstein. The New York Times for excerpts from HANK GREENBERG: THE STORY OF MY LIFE edited by Ira Berkow, 1989. Copyright © 1989 by The New York Times Company; and excerpts of quotes by Arthur Daley from THE NEW YORK TIMES BOOK OF BASEBALL. ABC News for excerpts from episode entitled "Together and Apart, 1943" broadcast December 4, 1986. Courtesy ABC News OUR WORLD. William Mead for excerpts from EVEN THE BROWNS. Copyright © 1978 by William Mead. Published by Contemporary Book. Reprinted in 1985 by Farragut Publishing Company, Washington, D.C. SNS for excerpts from ESPN's Major League Baseball's Magazine's episode entitled "Baseball Goes to War." Courtesy Major League Baseball Productions.

Published by Crown Publishers, Inc.,
201 East 50th Street, New York, New York 10022.
Member of the Crown Publishing Group.
CROWN is a trademark of Crown Publishers, Inc.
Manufactured in the United States of America
Library of Congress Cataloging-in-Publication Data
Gilbert, Bill, 1931–
    They also served : baseball and the home front, 1941–1945 / Bill Gilbert.
    1. Baseball—United States—History.   I. Title.
    GV863.A1G55   1992
    796.357'0973—dc20   91-35813
                                                             CIP

ISBN 0-517-58522-7
Book Design by Shari deMiskey
10 9 8 7 6 5 4 3 2 1
F I R S T   E D I T I O N

CONTENTS

Part Three: 1943

Part Four: 1944

Part Five: 1945

THANK-YOUS

NO BOOK ABOUT THE PEOPLE AND THE TIMES FROM HALF A century ago is possible without the assistance of many persons in different capacities. I am pleased to express my deep thanks to the following men and women.

The baseball players themselves are at the top of my list. All were gracious and generous in talking with me and providing insight, information, humor, and drama for the telling of this story. For this and the pleasure of it all, I thank:

Lou Boudreau, Phil Cavarretta, Ellis Clary, Tony Cuccinello, Dom DiMaggio, Bob Feller, Rick Ferrell, Pete Gray, Tommy Henrich, Tommy Holmes, Whitey Kurowski, Buddy Lewis, Danny Litwhiler, Walter Masterson, Hal Newhouser, Mickey Owen, Bert Shepard, Cecil Travis, Johnny Vander Meer, Charlie Wagner, and Ted Williams.

The staff of the National Baseball Library at the Baseball Hall of Fame was extremely helpful, as always—Bill Deane, the senior research associate; his intern, Sean Rooney; and

Pat Kelly, the library's photo collection manager. Fern Solomon at the Montgomery County (Maryland) Public Library and the staff at the National Archives in Washington also provided valuable assistance.

Special thanks are also due Shirley Povich, the baseball writer and columnist of the *Washington Post,* whose willingness to give me his autograph innocently led me into the world of journalism after World War II.

Other members of the media also shared wartime experiences or information with me—Billy Rowe, then a columnist for the *Pittsburgh Courier,* Willie Weinbaum and Mike Kostel of the Phoenix Communications Group, producers of "Major League Baseball Magazine." Another TV program, ABC's "Our World," was a helpful source for which I thank Walter Porges, vice president of news practices for ABC News, and hosts Linda Ellerbee and Ray Gandolf and their staff. Two fellow authors, who wrote the most informative and entertaining books on baseball during this period—Bill Meade, author of *Even the Browns* (since reprinted in a paperback edition as *Baseball Goes to War*), and Richard Goldstein, who wrote *Spartan Seasons,* deserve special mention.

Lillian Gilbert and Dave Gilbert performed their usual excellent services in aiding with research and editing. Bob Gregoire thoughtfully lent me his priceless wartime magazines and other publications from his extensive collection of baseball information and memorabilia items. Ed Liberatore—again—was a valuable communications link with many of the players listed above and a source of rich stories of his own from these years.

Joyce Engelson, my editor at Crown Publishers, proved she is as knowledgeable about baseball as she is about editing, so this book is better on both counts. An extra expression of gratitude is always due to the man who finds a publisher for me first and gets mentioned last, my agent and a vice president of the Scott Meredith Literary Agency, Russell Galen.

MAJOR LEAGUE BASEBALL AT THE START OF WORLD WAR II

American League

BOSTON RED SOX
Owner: Tom Yawkey
Manager: Joe Cronin
Home: Fenway Park

NEW YORK YANKEES
Owner: Estate of Colonel
Jacob Ruppert
Manager: Joe McCarthy
Home: Yankee Stadium

CHICAGO WHITE SOX
Owner: Grace Comiskey
Manager: Jimmy Dykes
Home: Comiskey Park

PHILADELPHIA ATHLETICS
Owner and Manager:
Connie Mack
Home: Shibe Park

CLEVELAND INDIANS
Owner: Alva Bradley
Manager: Lou Boudreau
Home: League Park

ST LOUIS BROWNS
Owner: Don Barnes
Manager: Luke Sewell
Home: Sportsman's Park

DETROIT TIGERS
Owner: Walter "Spike" Briggs
Manager: Del Baker
Home: Briggs Stadium

WASHINGTON SENATORS
Owner: Clark Griffith
Manager: Bucky Harris
Home: Griffith Stadium

National League

BOSTON BRAVES
Owner: Bob Quinn
Manager: Casey Stengel
Home: Braves Field

BROOKLYN DODGERS
Owner: Estate of Charles Ebbets
Manager: Leo Durocher
Home: Ebbets Field

CHICAGO CUBS
Owner: Phil Wrigley
Manager: Jimmie Wilson
Home: Wrigley Field

CINCINNATI REDS
Owner: Powell Crosley, Jr.
Manager: Bill McKechnie
Home: Crosley Field

NEW YORK GIANTS
Owner: Horace Stoneham
Manager: Mel Ott
Home: Polo Grounds

PHILADELPHIA PHILLIES
Owner: Gerald Nugent
Manager: Hans Lobert
Home: Shibe Park

PITTSBURGH PIRATES
Owner: Mrs. Barney Dreyfuss
Manager: Frankie Frisch
Home: Forbes Field

ST. LOUIS CARDINALS
Owner: Sam Breadon
Manager: Billy Southworth
Home: Sportsman's Park

BASEBALL'S CHAMPIONS DURING
WORLD WAR II

Pennant Winners

American League	Year	National League
New York Yankees	1942	St. Louis Cardinals
New York Yankees	1943	St. Louis Cardinals
St. Louis Browns	1944	St. Louis Cardinals
Detroit Tigers	1945	Chicago Cubs

World Series Winners

1942 St. Louis Cardinals
1943 New York Yankees
1944 St. Louis Cardinals
1945 Detroit Tigers

Batting

American League	Year	National League
Ted Williams, .356 Boston Red Sox	1942	Ernie Lombardi, .330 Boston Braves
Luke Appling, .328 Chicago White Sox	1943	Stan Musial, .357 St. Louis Cardinals
Lou Boudreau, .327 Cleveland Indians	1944	Dixie Walker, .357 Brooklyn Dodgers
George Stirnweiss, .309 New York Yankees	1945	Phil Cavarretta, .355 Chicago Cubs

Pitching (most wins)

American League	Year	National League
Tex Hughson, 22 Boston Red Sox	1942	Mort Cooper, 22 St. Louis Cardinals
Spud Chandler and Dizzy Trout, 20 New York Yankees	1943	Mort Cooper, Elmer Riddle, and Rip Sewell, 21 Cincinnati Reds
Hal Newhouser, 29 Detroit Tigers	1944	Bucky Walters, 23 Cincinnati Reds
Hal Newhouser, 25 Detroit Tigers	1945	Red Barrett, 23 Boston Braves/St. Louis Cardinals

Most Valuable Players

American League	Year	National League
Joe Gordon New York Yankees	1942	Mort Cooper St. Louis Cardinals
Spud Chandler New York Yankees	1943	Stan Musial St. Louis Cardinals
Hal Newhouser Detroit Tigers	1944	Marty Marion St. Louis Cardinals
Hal Newhouser Detroit Tigers	1945	Phil Cavarretta Chicago Cubs

Part One

1941

A BATBOY'S MEMORIES

WAS IT REALLY FIFTY YEARS AGO?

. . . Since Joe DiMaggio's fifty-six-game hitting streak produced almost as many headlines as the approach of World War II?

. . . Since Ted Williams became the last player to reach the magic level of a .400 batting average, while the Japanese prepared to attack Pearl Harbor?

Has it been half a century since Bob Feller, the winningest pitcher in baseball for the previous three years—and just turned twenty-three—put aside his draft deferment as the sole support of his dying father, his mother, and kid sister to join the Navy two days after Pearl Harbor?

. . . And since Hank Greenberg, discharged from the Army on December 5, reentered four days later?

Has it been half a century since five hundred other major-league baseball players and another four thousand minor leaguers marched off, sailed off, and flew off on journeys to faraway places with strange-sounding names like Guadalcanal and Iwo Jima, Salerno and Bastogne? Since they were

3

followed—but not really replaced—by players who were clas-
sifed "4-F" in the military draft, deferred because of physical
problems, including a one-armed outfielder and a one-
legged war hero, plus players in their midteens and men in
their late forties?

As America marks the fiftieth anniversary of that era,
which is more and more being called "America's last popular
war," we reopen a unique chapter in the 150-year bond
between baseball and us. It is one that no future generation
will be able to experience because our wars are different
now, and so are the public's opinions about them.

Those years and baseball's integral role in them form a
story worth remembering if you were a slightly bewildered
ten-year-old at the time of Pearl Harbor, as I was. If you
weren't around then, as grown-up or child, the story has
even more value in its retelling because it is unique.

The adults were alternately scared and confident, dis-
couraged and optimistic, weary and exhilarated. We kids felt
the same full range of emotions in our confused, uncertain
state, compounded by the tenderness of our years.

But all of us, kids and grown-ups, had one steadying ele-
ment that helped to hold our lives together, giving us a badly
needed sense of continuity and stability, something that even
a world war couldn't take from us—baseball.

No less than the president of the United States, Franklin
Roosevelt himself, said baseball was too important to us to be
stopped because of the war. In fact, he said more than that.
He said baseball could even help us *win* the war, because it
would be a strong force in improving the morale of our men
and women in uniform. FDR said baseball would give all
Americans, including those of us on "the home front," something to cheer about, an interest that would take our minds
off the war. He didn't say it about any other sport.

In the eventful and formative years that belong to the very
young, fate gave me a double view of that parade of events
that few teens or preteens were allowed to experience. I was
growing up in the city where our nation's survival was being
decided—Washington, D.C. The war news came from my
hometown as much as from the battlefields overseas.

And in the biggest thrill any kid can feel in either war or

4

peace, I became a major-league batboy in 1945, the last year of the war, proving that by then we suffered from more than just a manpower shortage—we had a *boypower* shortage, too.

It was a rare time, but it was a hard time, too—men and women by the millions going off to war, twelve million before it was all over, and the rationing of such essential items as meat and sugar and gas (you were allowed only three gallons a week for your car). German submarines were sinking American ships so close to our East Coast that residents of beach towns from New England to Florida could see our ships go down, and Japanese "balloon bombs" landed on the West Coast.

Hope and Crosby clowned and sang with Dorothy Lamour in their first "road" picture, and Kate Smith sang "God Bless America." A hollow-cheeked kid from New Jersey named Frank Sinatra attracted a mob scene of "bobby-soxers" when he appeared at the Paramount Theater in New York, and the new comedy team of Abbott and Costello performed a baseball routine that still has Americans asking "Who's on first?"

Roosevelt and Thomas Dewey opposed each other in a wartime presidential election, and John L. Lewis pulled his coal miners off the job despite organized labor's no-strike pledge at the start of the war. Dreaded polio epidemics spread their fear and tragedy every summer. The newspapers published a casualty list every day, which you checked to see if you knew any of the dead, wounded, or missing in action. We experienced frequent air-raid drills and blackouts, and people stood on wooden observation towers, holding binoculars to their eyes trying to spot approaching enemy bombers—maybe wondering how much good it would do to spot them if the planes were already in binocular range.

In baseball, too, life was different. One of the star pitchers, who was so good he remained a star in the postwar competition, Hal Newhouser, was declared 4-F because of a heart condition, even though he tried to enlist and become a pilot. That didn't stop one fan from sending him a one-word letter—"Bastard"—on yellow paper.

The St. Louis Browns, who had never won a pennant before, won the American League flag in 1944 mainly because they escaped damage from the military draft that year better than most other teams. It was the only pennant they ever won. The next year, the Chicago Cubs won the pennant in the National League. They haven't won one since.

Major-league teams trained in the north because of wartime restrictions on unnecessary travel. Instead of the warm breezes and swaying palms of Florida and Arizona, they were training in snow and cold near Boston, Chicago, New York, and other northern cities.

Men and women in military uniform got into games free. Most of baseball's owners and players voluntarily took 10 percent of their salaries in war bonds to do their part to help pay for the war effort. Fans actually threw foul balls back onto the field so they could be shipped to military bases for "the boys" to enjoy.

The war produced some of the best of the postwar crop of big-league players—Newhouser, Stan Musial, Johnny Pesky, George Kell, Allie Reynolds, Dave "Boo" Ferriss, Eddie Lopat, "Snuffy" Stirnweiss, and Hank Sauer. Two teenagers who got a chance to play in the big leagues because of the war, Ed Yost and Joe Nuxhall, made good after the war too and became stars.

But the men who really kept the sport alive for our national morale—and for "our fighting men overseas"—were the 4-Fs, and kids like Yost and Nuxhall, plus the one-armed outfielder, Pete Gray, and Ellis Clary, "Bingo" Binks, Nap Reyes, Danny Gardella, and the draft-exempt Cubans on the Washington Senators—Gil Torres, Alejandro Carrasquel, Bobby Estalella, and Roberto Ortiz.

It was a time when one of history's greatest home-run hitters, Jimmie Foxx, became a pitcher. Another pitcher, Hod Lisenbee, born during the Spanish-American War, returned after nine years of retirement and pitched in thirty-one games for the Cincinnati Reds. Pepper Martin left four years of retirement to play in forty games for his old team, the St. Louis Cardinals, at the age of forty, hit .279, and helped the Cards win their third straight National League pennant.

Maybe the kids and the 4-Fs weren't the greatest players baseball fans ever paid to see, and maybe the old-timers were imitations of their former greatness, but for four seasons beginning in 1942, they were our favorites. They were the ones whose exploits we cheered, whose shortcomings we

6

overlooked, and whose contributions to the war effort quali-
fied them to feel that, in a manner considered important
even by the president, they also served.

Whatever they lacked in talent, the wartime teams provided four years of entertainment that other seasons have
not always matched: one of the biggest upsets in World
Series history in 1942, the first night All-Star Game in 1943,
pennant races in the American League decided on the last
day of the 1944 season and again in '45, Newhouser's fifty-
four wins in two seasons and his back-to-back Most Valuable
Player awards, the only pitcher to win the prize two years in a
row. Wartime baseball wasn't all incompetence and pratfalls,
although we had our share of that, too.

The war produced heroes and victims in baseball—like
Bert Shepard of the Washington Senators, whose experiences as a fighter pilot, amputee, prisoner of war, and a
big-league baseball player pitching on an artificial leg ex-
emplify those years and this book. Two other baseball players, no better known than Shepard, were also heroes in
World War II. They played a total of six games in the major
leagues, but were heroes nevertheless because they never
came back. They were the two major-league players who
gave their last full measure of devotion, an outfielder for the
Senators in five games before the war, named Elmer Ge-
deon, who died on a battlefield in France in 1944 five days
after his twenty-seventh birthday, and Harry O'Neill, a catcher for one game with the Philadelphia A's before the war,
who never came to bat and was killed on the sands of Iwo
Jima in 1945.

And there's the story of Moe Berg, the veteran catcher and
veteran spy, too, who played a critical cloak-and-dagger role
for our intelligence agency before the war in Japan and
during the war in Europe.

One of the war's most tragic victims wasn't killed or
wounded. He was another Senator, Cecil Travis, a perennial
all-star shortstop who was trapped with thousands of other
American troops in Europe's Battle of the Bulge at Christ-
mastime, 1944. Baseball people from that era unanimously
agree that Bastogne ended his baseball career prematurely,
although Travis modestly disagrees.

7

The wartime players weren't the only ones who were serving our nation through baseball. In New York, a one-of-a-kind campaign to sell war bonds raised well over one hundred million dollars through an "auction" of players from the city's three big-league teams. In Washington, columnist Shirley Povich of the *Post* turned promoter for a night and staged an exhibition game between the Senators and a team of ex-major-league players in the Navy, and raised enough money in war bonds to build a warship.

The Baseball Writers' Association of America cooperated with the big-league teams in a "Keep 'Em Slugging" campaign that raised enough funds to pay for 18,000 baseballs and 4,500 bats for our military bases in the early days of the war. Clark Griffith, Washington's owner, was instrumental in the effort, saying the equipment would be "the best we can get—none of that cheap stuff for the soldiers and sailors. Only the best for them."

Older people in baseball knew Mr. Griffith wasn't kidding. Exactly twenty-five years earlier, in 1917, he had done the same thing for the soldiers and sailors of World War I.

Washington, which grew into its present role as the capital of the free world during and after World War II, was also the site for many of the baseball events during these years and the operating base for many of the personalities in this story. That, plus my own presence here and my job as a spring-training batboy—one barely able to lift a major-league bat much less swing one—accounts for the many stories about Washington, its scenes and its people during the war.

Through it all, baseball changed. At the same time, its grip on us grew even stronger and more enduring, giving the sport the special place in our lives that enabled it to survive and prosper later, even through the tumult of recent years with seven-figure salaries, free agents, strikes, lockouts, and the fall from grace of the man with the most base hits in history.

This is not just a baseball story—although it is that—but a different view, in a unique context, of World War II as we lived it on the home front. That's why the story of those four years is worth telling now to those too young to have lived through them and retelling to those of us who did.

We're Fighting for a Lot of Things in This War, and Baseball Is One of Them.

A wounded American soldier, 1944

1

A TEN-YEAR-OLD'S WORLD

IN 1941, THE FEAR OF A SECOND WORLD WAR SEEMED TO BE the only thing most adults talked to each other about, except for Joe DiMaggio's fifty-six-game hitting streak and the .406 batting average of Ted Williams. When you're just a skinny ten-year-old kid and your parents and their friends are talking about a war coming, sometimes it worries you. Other times, you pay more attention to the really important things in life, like baseball.

That's what millions of Americans did, and not just ten-year-olds, and baseball responded magnificently by providing us with its most historic season. In addition to Joe's streak and Ted's average, there was Ted's dramatic home run with two outs in the bottom of the ninth inning in Detroit to win the All-Star Game for the American League, plus Tommy Henrich's strikeout that wasn't a strikeout in the World Series when he and Brooklyn's catcher, Mickey Owen, both missed a third-strike curve ball from Hugh Casey. Tommy reached first base, the Yankees staged a two-out, ninth-inning rally and won the game that day and the Series the next.

11

It was a season to remember at a time when we were trying to forget, forget the coming war and enjoy baseball every chance we got. And what a year to enjoy, except for men like Hugh Mulcahy.

Mulcahy was a big right-handed pitcher for the Philadelphia Phillies, six feet two inches and 190 pounds. His misfortune was to be pitching for one of the worst teams in baseball, a team that finished no higher than next-to-last, and usually last, in his six prewar seasons with them beginning in 1935.

With the Phillies losing more than one hundred games a year, Hugh led the National League in losses twice—twenty defeats in 1938 and twenty-two in 1940. Even though he achieved the impossible by winning ten games with the Phillies in '38 and thirteen in 1940, he acquired a nickname that no other player has ever wanted—"Losing Pitcher" Mulcahy.

Not long after President Roosevelt went on the radio with one of his "fireside chats" and told us, "Never before has our American civilization been in such danger as now," Mulcahy became the first major-league baseball player to be drafted. He was inducted into the Army on March 8, 1941, as one of the new members of the 101st Artillery at Camp Edwards on Cape Cod. He was twenty-seven years old, a prime age for any professional athlete.

On reporting to camp, he told reporters, "It might be a little tougher and might take a little longer for me to get into shape when I report for spring training next season, but I don't think this year of Army life will hamper my pitching any."

He even went one better, adding, "Personally I think this conscription bill is a great thing for the young men of today." He said his only regret was that he had not been able to finish making the payments on the new home he had bought for his parents in the Boston suburb of Newton.

For the first time, a caption writer composed a line that was destined to became a wartime cliché. Next to a picture of Mulcahy, the New York *Daily News* caption hailed him:

PITCHING FOR UNCLE SAM!

The expectation, or at least the hope, was that our young men would be gone for a year. That's what the law said at the time. A songwriter made the most of it with a 1939–1940 hit, "Good-bye, Dear—I'll Be Back in a Year."

As events unfolded, the length of sevice was made indefinite—the duration of the war and six months, abbreviated in conversation to "the duration and six." Mulcahy missed spring training in 1942, also 1943, '44, and '45. He returned near the end of the '45 season, and was able to pitch in only twenty-three more games before retiring in 1947.

Phil Rizzuto's hopes of making the grade with his hometown team as a rookie with the New York Yankees received a severe jolt eleven days after Mulcahy was inducted. At the Yankees' spring-training camp in St. Petersburg, Florida, Rizzuto was informed that he had been reclassified 1-A in the draft—fit for military service.

Dr. Frederick Kumm of the St. Petersburg draft board, after a preliminary exam revealed Rizzuto might have diabetes, said a second urinalysis showed the first reading was "due to excitement," according to one newspaper account. "The recheck this morning," the article said, "proved that Phil last night had become quite nervous over the examination."

There was reason for concern at the Rizzuto family home back at 7801 64th Street in Brooklyn's Glendale section. Phil was the primary support of his parents, a kid brother, and himself. Without Phil's salary as a rookie major leaguer, the family would have to get by on his father's salary as a night watchman—twenty dollars a week.

Near the end of spring training the rookie was reclassified again, this time 3-A as the main support of his family. He entered the Navy after the 1942 season and served for three years.

The Yankees weren't overly concerned, even though they said they didn't want to lose a rookie of Rizzuto's potential. President Ed Barrow told reporters, "It would be tough to lose Rizzuto, who is one of the greatest young shortstops I have seen in fifty years. However, we have a big job to do in this country and ball players cannot expect favors. . . . Personally, I refuse to get excited about ball players and the draft."

13

As spring training neared its end, our Washington Senators, still called the Nats by many as short for Nationals, their other nickname, beat the Detroit Tigers for the seventh straight time in a rainy spring-training game in Greenville, South Carolina.

Five days later, FDR opened the 1941 major-league season, throwing out the traditional first ball at Washington's Griffith Stadium for the eighth time as president. He even threw it out once when he wasn't president. That was back in 1917 when he was assistant secretary of the Navy and President Woodrow Wilson was preoccupied with our entry into World War I.

In '41 it was our right-handed knuckleball ace, Dutch Leonard, versus the Yankees and one of their left-handers, Marius Russo. While FDR greeted well-wishers in the presidential box next to the Washington dugout on the first-base side, Vice President Henry Wallace and the Nats' owner, Clark Griffith, led the traditional march to the flagpole in center field.

The temperature was eighty-eight degrees, and most of the fans were in shirtsleeves. The atmosphere was upbeat due to the warm April sunshine and the eagerness of the 32,000 fans to forget the war in Europe and the growing threat of America's involvement. Instead they were interested in enjoying baseball in the sunshine and the pleasing aroma of fresh bread coming down from the Bond Bakery just above the ballpark on Georgia Avenue. The headline in the *Washington Post* the next morning captured the mood:

WAR CLOUDS ARE FORGOTTEN

AS THRONG HAILS PRESIDENT

In keeping with another sacred baseball tradition, there were no other games played that day. Major-league baseball showcased itself by allowing the Nats, or the Senators, to start every season at home, with no other games in either league except those seasons when the Cincinnati Reds, as the sport's oldest professional team, might open the National League season the same day. But Washington always had the Amer-

14

ican League opener for itself, and often the entire baseball stage.

With the president always there—beginning with William Howard Taft in 1910, until the Senators were hustled out of town to Texas by Bob Short after the 1971 season the year before he sold them—baseball reaped a publicity bonanza each April, thanks to its association with the Oval Office.

It's something no other sport has accomplished even once for an opening day. No president ever threw out the first football of the season or the first basketball or the first hockey puck. In baseball, with a team in Washington, it happened every spring.

In 1941, one of Washington's rookie pitchers, Arnold (Red) Anderson, caught FDR's opening toss. That was an improvement over the year before, when Roosevelt's presidential pitch hit a *Washington Post* camera and smashed it. As the former manager of his prep school baseball team at Groton, FDR seemed to have lost a little of his control.

The outcome of the game was also traditional—3–0, Yankees. Leonard held the Yankees to only six hits, but the Nats got only three off Russo. Joe DiMaggio began his historic 1941 performance with a triple over Doc Cramer's head in center field to drive in the first run of the season.

Anne Hagner reported in the *Post* the next morning that a woman going to the opening game found herself in a dilemma. "To look feminine or be comfortable," she wrote, "is the choice she must make—and you'd be amazed at the number of them who prefer the former."

She said knowledgeable women wear "sports frocks and low heels." She said others dress in a "floppy hat, a sheer print, and expensive nylon hose."

By the time the next opening day arrived, President Roosevelt would be unavailable—and so would nylons.

2

FREIGHT TRAIN TO
A BETTER LIFE

IN THE TINY FARMING COMMUNITY OF CLINTON, INDIANA—
population 2,500—the grim future facing the world early in
1941 wasn't enough to dim the enthusiasm of a strapping
twenty-one-year-old tenant farmer's son named Bert Shepard.

He was a minor-league baseball player, and the biggest
problem facing him wasn't the war—it was how to improve
his control as a left-handed pitcher so he could make it to the
big leagues. Young Bert had no way of knowing that events
to come in 1941 would start a series of developments that
would change his life forever and would, incidentally, bring
us together four years later in a way that no Hollywood
scriptwriter could have imagined.

For young Bert, with his roots in America's heartland, life
was definitely getting better and his enthusiastic, positive
nature was easier to maintain. The hard times of the Great
Depression, which wasn't great at all to anyone who lived
through it, were felt as keenly on Clinton's Main Street as on
New York's Wall Street, but those bad old days of the 1930s
were receding for Lura and John Shepard and their six sons.

And Bert, their second son, was making good money as a baseball player—sixty dollars a month.

The family had moved from Dana Bert's birthplace, also the hometown of a man whose name would become a household word in the war that was on the horizon—Ernie Pyle. He became America's best-known and -loved war correspondent—yes, a correspondent who was *loved* by the public—and he was from right there in Dana, seventy miles due west of Indianapolis on Highway 36, only ten miles from the Indiana-Illinois line. The whole town wasn't any bigger than some of the crowds Bert pitched in front of—750 people.

Bert's dad had a "delivery business"—a horse and a wagon—before the Depression took it away from him. Then he became a farmhand at a salary of fifty dollars a month plus a house for Lura and their boys. It was a transient existence, and as a youngster Bert lived in thirteen different communities. And yes, they really did walk four miles one way in all kinds of weather to a one-room schoolhouse for the first eight grades.

In the first full year of the Depression, 1930, Bert was sent to live with his grandmother in her small home across the street from the train depot. She was one of the fortunate town folks who owned a radio, and through that magic box Bert learned about baseball games and their stars, especially Pepper Martin and the St. Louis Cardinals.

In the mid-1930s, Bert, now in his early teens, began hanging around the high school baseball team, watching its practices, shagging fly balls, chasing foul ones, and doing anything and everything to stay close to the sport that was becoming his lifelong love. He didn't even mind that he had to cover those four miles home after practice by running all the way because it was dark by then.

As his high school years unfolded, folks began to see that the second oldest boy in the Shepard family was becoming a good baseball player, starring in sandlot games around their new hometown of Clinton.

Life was getting easier for him in other ways. He taught himself how to cut hair and became known as "the traveling barber," giving haircuts in people's homes for ten cents. One family was an especially lucrative account—a father and six

17

kids. With that seventy cents, the young man who was blossoming into a sure-enough ball player could treat himself to a White Castle hamburger for a nickel, a chocolate malt for another nickel, and a trip to the movies for a dime, and still have some money left to give to his mother.

Things were improving for his father, too. He was able to save up and buy a Model T Ford—for five dollars. He drove it for two years and then made a hefty profit by selling it for seven dollars.

Baseball's lure proved too strong for Bert by the end of his junior year in high school in 1937. He'd heard that California was the place to go if you wanted to be a baseball player. The weather was good all year long, so there were more teams, more games, and more chances to become good enough to make it as a professional ball player.

With a pal, Bert hopped a freight train out of Clinton bound for Terre Haute, then found another that went all the way to St. Louis. As a paternal send-off, Bert's father provided the strongest financial support he could by giving his son all the money he had in the world—fifty cents.

Bert's odyssey included ten days in jail in Amarillo, Texas, after railroad detectives spotted him, prompting him to hitchhike the rest of the trip. He made it to California by working along the way as a busboy in restaurants to get his meals and a few cents to finance the next leg of his journey.

In California, a job at a tire retread plant at ten dollars a week for a six-day week supported him while he played baseball on every playground and in every league he could find. With that steady salary, he could even afford a copy of *Life* magazine when it published a spread of pictures showing the pitching form of Johnny Vander Meer of Cincinnati in 1938, when he became the only man ever to pitch two consecutive no-hit games. From those pictures and with the mirror in his rooming house, Bert was able to teach himself the crude elements of a pitcher's windup.

With his newly gained prosperity and realizing the importance of a good education—it was becoming harder to get ahead in life without a high school diploma—Bert bought a bus ticket home, worked as a barber in a camp of the Civilian Conservation Corps, and made thirty dollars a month. When